REVENANCE

REVENANCE

poems

Cynthia Hogue

RED HEN PRESS | *Pasadena, CA*

Book design and layout by Li Pallas and Jaimie Evans

Cover design by Mark E. Cull

Library of Congress Cataloging-in-Publication Data

Revenance : poems / Cynthia Hogue.—First edition.

   pages cm

 ISBN 978-1-59709-541-9 (paperback)

 I. Title.

 PS3558.O34754A6 2014

 811'.54—dc23

               2014019061

The National Endowment for the Arts, the Los Angeles County Arts Commission, the Los Angeles Department of Cultural Affairs, the Pasadena Arts & Culture Commission and the City of Pasadena Cultural Affairs Division, and Sony Pictures Entertainment partially support Red Hen Press.

First Edition

Published by Red Hen Press

www.redhen.org

ACKNOWLEDGMENTS

Thanks to the editors of the following journals for publishing individual poems, sometimes in earlier versions and with other titles: *American Letters & Commentary*, "austerity," "The Scroll"; *Barrow Street*, "The Mystery Is Belief," "Revenant (2)," "Spirit Says (1)"; *Blackbird*, "At the Lawrence Ranch," "Fluff," "Offhanded"; *The Common*, "Bounty," "Hiking South Mountain," "Spring in New Hampshire," "The Unfeeling"; *Court Green*, "Revenant (1)"; *Crazyhorse*, "At the Lawrence Tree," "On Securities and Exchange"; *Eclipse*, "The Woman Who Talked with Trees"; *Fiddlehead*, "In Evidence the Spring," "In New Hampshire Woods"; *Gestalt Review*, "Clearly in Fall"; *Great River Review*, "Vengeance"; *Hayden's Ferry Review*, "Interview with a Samizdat Poet"; *Hotel Amerika*, "The Blizzard," "Care Giving: An Elegy," "Sentimental"; *Interim*, "The Sibyl"; *Kestrel*, "In/Visible," "The Passivist," "The Walking Woman of Lewisburg, PA"; *Lo-Ball*, "In the Space-Time Studio of Morgan O"; *New American Writing*, "Spirit Says (2)"; *New Orleans Review*, "Small Mahogany Table with Voice"; *Superstition Review*, "The Cayadutta Creek Suite," "Elegy with Window," "On Principle"; *Third Coast Review*, "Foreclosure"; *Trickhouse*, "At the Agnes Martin Gallery."

"Here on Your Canvas" was included in *The Best of Toadlily Press: New & Selected Poems* edited by Myrna Goodman and Meredith Trede (Toadlily Press, 2011). "I Sit Here Writing" was solicited for a special issue on creativity published in *Gestalt Review*, edited by Susan L. Fischer (2009). "Fluff" was included in *The Ecopoetry Anthology* edited by Ann Fisher-Wirth and Laura-Gray Street (Trinity UP, 2013), in an earlier version. "Spring in New Hampshire" was featured on *Verse Daily* on December 31, 2012. "in the meadow magenta" was featured on *Poem-a-Day* by Text Television in collaboration with the Academy of American Poets on January 30, 2013. "Elegy with Boulder," "Elegy with Lake," "The Place of Feelings," were published in "A Poetry Congeries," curated by John Hoppenthaler for *Connotation Press: An Online Artifact* (June 2013).

A sabbatical leave from the Department of English at Arizona State University provided me with the time to begin this book. Residency fellowships from the MacDowell Colony, the Helene M. Wurlitzer Foundation of New Mexico, and the Santa Fe Art Institute gave me quiet spaces in which to advance this book. I am grateful to these organizations, their directors, and the incredible artists I met during my residencies—truly an inspiration. Let me express my thanks to the publishers and founding editors of Red Hen Press, the writers Kate Gale and Mark Cull, for their continued support and the beautiful books they make. To the friends and colleagues who have helped me in innumerable ways with this book, here a few by name: Devreaux Baker, Jan Beatty, Martha Collins, Norman Dubie, Kathleen Fraser, Scott Hightower, Alan Michael Parker, Stephen O'Connor, Alicia Ostriker, Karl Patten, Alberto Rios, Jeannine Savard, and Afaa Weaver. Profound gratitude to Karen Brennan, Christopher Burawa, and Elizabyth Hiscox for timely, crucial reads of this book in manuscript draft. Finally, to my husband, Sylvain Gallais: *without your love nothing is possible.*

In memory of Earl Hogue (1925–2011)
and Evangeline Erickson Hogue (1925–2013)

Love is like Life — merely longer
—Emily Dickinson

∞

. . . As the dry ears are laid to be stored
through the season when the fields lie barren,
                                    this is the time
                                    this is the evidence
of the time when one travels to the cemeteries and addresses
the Lord of the Dead.
—Mark Nowak

Table of Contents

IV

V

REVENANCE

I

In Evidence the Spring

She overslept the hours,
was ravenous for
an extravagance of reason
when all changed

Fiddleheads furled
deliberatively, close to the leaf-
bed—muddled—with other
rare stem and petal

She gathered them
to dream one or the other
that bordered
the dangered   These facts

she found:
a rickety, wraparound
porch with
hanging planters of pink impatiens

She was alone by then,
feeling huge,
all mouth
That hunger is not   necessarily

an accident even though
called one
puzzled her for she confessed
no   understanding of consequence

or the difference a word   made
Extinction of the bright
                       greenness
before her offered no proof

In New Hampshire Woods

That an owl hooted.
No glimpse of wing:

time marked
in sound that seemed misheard.

More hoots, solo and sonorous.
They're speaking in tones

that differ as chords
from words, you said. The heavens

vanished behind trees
in stark outline. Starlight

stuttered. Then a distant car
I thought a growl and felt the cold stone,

a prickle of nettles, the sweet rose-
scent of honeysuckle: insensible, audible

minutes slipped intransigently past us
in a rising flitter of syllable.

I Sit Here Writing

The poem is cerebral. Its writing physical.
—Virginie Lalucq

It was evening then it wasn't.
I wrote huddled, unsleeping,
pissing next door, not
eating, unbathed. Words came forth

in a gush like blood.
There was no pain—
nothing like that—
more like the concentration it takes

for water to become
ice. I fainted once,
woke up on the floor.
Maybe I imagined it.

The crush of air and spirits around me,
voices murmuring nothing
I understood, made my breath catch.
I licked my lips, suddenly thirsty.

The words were poems.
I knew no more my fate
than when I was born: whether
when I arrived I'd have been

going there all along. There's no
there though. There's just here.
Hello. Morning's limpid, lumin-
ous, the sky not yet not dark,

stars still, even Venus
which I consider without interest,
the silence a curse of linden
bursting silver, and the light slivering.

in the meadow magenta

(reading Robert Duncan in Haldon Forest)

bloom looks
like lupine from afar
but up close the small bell-
like flowers of wild hollyhock

the holy that forth
came that must

come mystery
of frond fern
gorse a magic
to which I

relate to
landof hillock and

bolder the grayer
sky and wood
the straight flat One
between them barred

by the bushy Scots pine
medicinal veridian of ever-

green which though
gossip rumor spell
or chance change us
is not changed

Spirit Says (1)

Granite. Says, lapidary.
Polish you with breeze on which it travels
that you cannot glaze or fix. What con-

traption feels familiar
as in kind? The curl-
icue and whirligig. Sputter,

mutter back. Spells
binding with the act of them:
will break you so don't brake

or call Time out when Space uncovers
all the layers sedimented like a midden
that is "you," brushes off sand stoppers of

the bottled up. Chisels marbled
memory which shivers
into pieces, flecked. This numinously.

Spirit Says (2)

Voice of
or *voice for*
which is *a capacity to change*

one word and all
meaning: Why words are used
to sing or cheat

How words can work at all
Right now writes words:
say, *bone* or *round,*

the tone or sound
which shifts the note that's struck—
long "o" for grief

The open "ou"
of pained surprise a modification:
"the change of a vowel

brought about by assimilation"
to another: The being next to one
letter changes both—

That next-to-ness that makes new
sounds, trans-
formed: all fixity vanishing

We talk *around* the words
or *through* them
That we lie develops

our ability to read *between*
the words—and even falsehoods
carry forth a tenor which re-

sonates air, vibrates
delicately in ripples outwards:
a quaver that avers

The Woman Who Talked with Trees

That a tree could speak:
That a woman claiming

to converse with and to
tell the story of trees in

a novel she hides
in her desk so careful

to talk *about* but otherwise
to keep tree-

speech to herself
walked into a stand of vernal

elm, endangered oak,
and spoke: *To*

you and you
listened to her. In that grove,

those trees now conjured
that words would keep them.

Spring in New Hampshire

1

A whooshing passed over us —
and perched on a branch — something
see-sawed in the bright dark air,

sailed the clearing sharp-
eyed through pole pine sapling,
beech, maple and hemlock

Blake says are threatened beyond saving:
"Once we were too far north to worry
about infestations but now we must,

I guess: Earth's breath is fast as hyper-
ventilation, and no one —
not even scientists — knows why

or what will come."
I tell him spirits we walk among
steal glasses (last week mine

whisked off and weirdly
found soon after in New York),
or frizzle our lines

until they squiggle
and we wonder what we've made
or if it can be fixed.

2

Yesterday, I watched an ant hauling
a burden across the drive before me.
It dropped the object

to trek in ever-widening circles,
coming back to resume the task
once it had found the way all clear.

The ant built small piles of spruce
needles to camouflage its find which,
when I went to look, was a spider

too big for the anthill's opening.
That had to be dug out.
I showed Blake when he stopped,

who carried with him
two books on animal symbols, the ant
being patience and the spider creativity

(though maybe not a dead spider).
Later I found beside the entrance
the ant excavated for hours

a little mound of dirt and both
ant and spider crushed by a car.
Today: no trace that they had been.

3

Blake will not speak of ghosts.
He'll talk of animals, trees, weather
and angels but only briefly.
Spirits are not the same

as ghosts and angels of course
are very rare, didn't I know that?
                              He has to go.
. At night, down the alley of trees
the low-reaching, feather-like boughs

suture the air as we draw
the efflorescence from this wound
on which the world's stretched
before us teal and oily like a sea.

II

Interview with a Samizdat Poet

When I was not a human being
I saw rivers and thought,
What is water for?
　　—Olga Sedakova

Interview with a Samizdat Poet (1999/2011)

One never really thinks about a conversation as a piece forming a whole entity, unless the exchange was planned and plans went awry: in this case, to record a formal interview on Russian poetry, which was lost because equipment malfunctioned. I tell you that what was lost was the record of a perfectly synergized exchange between the poet and her interlocutors, but you must take my word for it. I have nothing to prove it.

On September 15, 1999, my friend Slava and I interviewed the Russian poet Olga Sedakova, who came to prominence in the years before *perestroika* as a Samizdat poet published primarily by privately distributed mimeographs that were read, often memorized, passed along. Her poetry is inscrutable enough to mystify any censor, though since the end of the Soviet Union, she need no longer disguise her devout Christianity. In my memory, a beautiful, intuitive and profound conversation unfolded over the course of two hours. Sedakova was reverberantly thoughtful. The interview was full of the back-and-forth of questions and answers, follow-ups, the kind of dance of impulse and inspiration in an interview expressed in the musical notes of English spoken in Russian accents.

It is September 2011. I hold in my hand an artifact: what could be salvaged of this interview, a sheaf of twenty pages of spattered words separated by ellipses and hyphens. It looks like the script of an experimental play. Slava and I were so unlucky as to have each brought a tape recorder that broke when we tried to use it. Astonished, unbelieving, we were forced to resort to the third, a cheap backup brought along as an afterthought. It mangled the speech.

Now, twelve years later, I happen upon the interview manuscript and it gives me pause. Why do I pick it up? I don't know. Something about

Sedakova's abbreviated discussion of *ostranenie* (остранение) captures my attention as I idly peruse the scattered words. Or perhaps the scrap of passage about love and nothingness, since my father, as I already sense, will be dead by New Year. The language salvaged from the lost interview composes an artifact whose history—a few fabled hours of an autumn afternoon—was also lost. I begin to excavate the thing itself, uncovering its shards of language, which I unearth, recompose, because I want the reconstructed piece to confirm, by the very fact of its existence, that something that is no more once took *place*, bodied *forth*, returning like a *revenant:* not whole, but changed. Struck by an absence at once partial and absolute.

∞

Everything could be written down
because you would understand,
although perhaps differently,
how the meaning of words survives their context.
Yes.
They were so clear.
Yes.
(Use capital "T" when referring to Them).

∞

∞

Them was the first "big bug"
post-nuclear horror flick
that nobody understood
as allegory of Communist invasion.
"It's *Them*!" screamed a little girl
in the desert. Sugar attracted Them.
So you became a voice of dissidence?
Yes.

∞

∞

These nebulous and unconcretizable words
register flickering realities out of love
of freedom. They do this out of love,
without which we are useless.
The carnal aspect
of incarnation is what is most
resisted . . . Nothing,
which seems at once very abstract,

as nothing is,
and also very concrete, as in adding
the definite article:
   "the nothing that is."
Where do these words come from?
Is *nothing*: existential?
metaphysical? religious?
Yes.

∞

∞

So this knocking on the door at the end is . . . ?
This is the rain.
Is it not an allusion to history?
Yes. No.
The rain becomes a manifestation of
this amazing power to – rain –
which comes at the end.
The water is proof there is a God.

∞

∞

My grandmother was talking forever
to everything, to the cow, to flowers
(How are you today, flower?).
To the casserole she would say:
  "Please don't burn up. Be patient."
To make Objects come alive,
talk to Them until they talk back:
As if you were inside a fairy tale.

∞

III

Words are physical: words are nature and matter,
order of place, changing place and force. Words
exert pressure. They go straight ahead of meaning,
pressing at its sides: they sway themselves.
The poem is a swaying of words.
    —Jean-Luc Nancy

On Securities and Exchange

A river runs through
the painting.
    Its blue wash
sweeps across the whole foreground.
It narrows, meanders into the canyon.

Its currents are the same sky-blue
as the triangle of sky,
    and the sun casts
a bright strip edged in beryl
through hills hulking into hunter green.

You no longer feel safe in the country,
which has exchanged safety, securities
for insecurities:
    such pressing matters
distract you from painting.

Art's abstraction
    of what's real,
its refusal to face
facts like everyone else—
or this is the thing—

its complication of what is
is what confuses you. Does the river
flow toward you or away?
You spend all day
    not deciding.

The Scroll

Stippled beneath glass,
rippled with moisture or age –
unsigned –
on cloth, perhaps rice paper, battle
or ancient hunting scene: horses rearing,
men with bows and headdress, three-horse
chariots with only the drivers' hands
visible, lifting reins – *hya hya* –

One of the men holds a pinwheel-like
pennant. One of the riders turns with
arrow
poised, taking aim. A riderless horse
halts to look back at his rider,
also taking aim. Below
the row of men are busts of deer
and ducks, peacocks gazing
this way or that. Some squiggles.

Above the men are stylized, scalloped curtains
decorated with small dots, as if across a stage.
Wash
of white on black, negative
in pen and ink, or delicate
woodcut of abstracted forms with clear,
unbroken lines: curved for neck haunch
beak tunic wheel.

To be unable to say if the scene is of war or of sport, and to think that those phenomena surpasseth understanding –

In the Space-Time Studio of Morgan O

(in mind of the artist Morgan O'Hara's Italian studio, and for her)

∞

Take the stairs to
    her studio in the barn a vault-

        ing space of beveled light and oak beams gnarled

with a gray five centuries
    weathered. Listen to

        the ghost-geese, the ghost-pigs rooting below,

     and on Sun-
   days the large farm
family so boisterous
  on their sole
     day of repose:

       the generations' simulacra at communal meal. Here's solo:

∞

∞

one wall's
been primed then

washed black over which white lines curl like photo-

graphic negatives of
dendrites that un-

furl and coil across the space creating ground.

She is de-
claring: *I will*
you my time here
are my notes the daily
record of my hours:

in drawers of neatly stacked ledgers, small script on antique

rice paper. The
writing's so precise it
shapes how she marks
time in actions some as
incidental as a conversation turned

tutorial when track of
    time was lost and dark-
        ness fell so far from

           all lights which point to human presence: *the vital*

       movements she makes
     tangible in order to e-
lude figuration and
   abstraction through di-
      rect neural trans-

        porting of one move (say, ascending stairs) into another

∞

(*drawing*): focused multi-
      penciled the simul-
          taneous grace-

        ful lines of earth's
           moving swirling evan-
              escence which

              merge someone or some-
         thing (a susurrant forest,
       barbling stream) through

      an attentive self-
    forgetting in the in-
stant she transmits.

∞

AT THE LAWRENCE RANCH

San Cristobal, New Mexico

Inside the tulle of curtain
table with battered typewriter
                    boiled by –
                        someone – as
revenge (story's apocryphal)
Outside the tumble of cord
                        over stacked
wood and
            tumult of
untrammeled branch with
an arc above
            the peeling bark
Sturdy snow
pearling up on
                mountain
                    cliff
We have climbed the dirt road
past piñon, blue sage, to the old pine
"the tree-trunk there like a guardian
angel" – genus *Seriphidium* –
                        Nowhere's
the name of the inscrutable
        maker
                Marker
                    of plumed
and ribald solitude wherein
"close quarters tempers flared"

HERE ON YOUR CANVAS

after the painter, Jerry Carniglia

Those puffballs
        cloud poufs, whitish
                pucks outlined
in shading grays,
        flattened once
                (in Photoshop)
resuscitated (reinflated)
        back to circular,
                triangulative,
oblongated (smooth)
        colored-in space
                are lilies? ghosts?
grains of rice?
        these formal
                mutants in a realm
of shifting shapes:
        The ground from
                which abstractions
distill form
        has no telling
                logic without
magic—material-
        izing something
                out of nothing:
That found-
        ation moves
                beneath us all,

which when ad-
     justing our feet
          we discover the be-
dazzling a-
     symmetric—a crux
          in play, a *find*.

REVENANT (1)

The drape's voile
hung askew. A sycamore
sapling's half-visible with

crooked, stick-
like branch. Evenings a rose window, worm-
hole, gyre appears in the wood, not round,

exactly: tree limbs form mono-
chromatic tesserae darken to scar-
let shot through with the last

blue light as time
shifts to false account:
I'm more alert to hear

the door open to shadow
which is what
looms the instant I'm lost

in thought, and start.
It's said the seer knows —
let's say the way of things —

the phrase familiar if not
the sight, the not-
known's bitter ruse.

AT THE LAWRENCE TREE

San Cristobal, New Mexico

The sky mosaics
through undulant pine branch

Freeze-framed, dust-
caught, heart-stopped

Silence alone transmits
resonance of feelings on

old path to the chapel
of marble and quartz

Altar of wings (a phoenix-bird),
newly-strewn yellow petals

"There are so many ghosts here"
In the painting

"Nothing but sky left to paint"
Puzzle pieces of midnight

blue among the tree's mass,
the jittered spectral of stars

AT THE AGNES MARTIN GALLERY

Harwood Museum of Art, Taos

Here one says *Look between the lines*

Penciled straight in free form making "grid paintings" that run the canvas's length

---

Some lines evident from
      white or shadow-
            blue brush strokes that they track: light
blueblueblueblueblueblueblueblueblueblueblueblueblueblueblueblueblueblueblue
and white and off-
whitewhitewhitewhitewhitewhitewhitewhitewhitewhitewhitewhitewhitewhitewhitewhite

---

Striped paintings
I make a note of
what the method *looks like*
having no words for what – it is –

"Perfect Day" – I think –
      An abstraction of
           light off the
                horizon from
Taos Mesa in summer
      might characterize
            the line's relation to
                all the artist saw

                                    (all wrong)

          :

              If
           (*Beauty is the mystery of life*)

And
To have *a clear idea of how*
       to proceed is not a beautiful
            image but a direction

                          (not blank)

Then
(*In our minds there is awareness of perfection*)
       My imposing
            meaning differs from her realm: to see is

not to know the mind's dis-
position ar-
       ranged in lines cast across the canvas
           which she painted in confident strokes

all her life, "she" an immutable sign of
solitude, hardiness (and I'm told *joy*), a perfectly
       clear fable of the artist's labor
          to keep the painting free

of *things*: as evidence the lines
which are not her perception tra-
       versing space, and not translucent but of all things simply a-

                          (ligned)

Revenant (2)

Spanning her scalp, invisible hands,
cradling. She turns to fire,
overcome. Happens where suddenly,

alone. The face, she feels, close to hers.   *Whispers.*
She hears them at the hour of vespers.   Ludic,
the words are lies mellifluously webbed

through wrongs, music of a harsher wind,
belonging to (forgotten). Murmurs
muddle, slink over night's wall,

startle rivulet: meaning meaning's   missed.

THE MYSTERY IS BELIEF

Whirls you from intention
to be practical, flicks you

like a fly toward luck
(which might be good or bad),

sends you to a place where stealth
infiltrates beauty and elements

that burnish ironwood
trunks upend all plans.

Over the rise are ruins
in red rock foothills scaring you.

Your fear's so cunning that
you cannot tell which actual

thing courage braves
(skin crawls somatically).

You think God's
an empiricist's distortion of proof

walking the ground
upon which

prayer's incanted, held,
though you be godless.

Hiking South Mountain

Arid stick of trail, waving ocotillo: O mottled cactus branch pointing beyond the pictographs of water sources – sun-like spirals, deer drinking – you scan but cannot find. The eagle's come a second time to float on wind in slow circles of descent until he's ten feet overhead banking to look you straight in the eye: You look back curious, alert – he is *eagle-eyed*, words of which under the intent gaze of one eye you grasp full meaning – you the large living thing on the ground. The third time, your wife saw a shadow of wings sweep over the yard. What was *that?* You were looking at the clock while your wife spoke, and did not see the flit of an impression of moving darkness passing by, or maybe you'd have said.

BOUNTY

A dull glow in the room like a lamp,
a munificence of table, shine of roast,
potatoes, gleam of sweets,
and guests sitting down, laughter,

but the thirteenth one late. Cross.
Night overtook him, following
complicated directions, the road he confused
with another, or forgot, all bearings lost so,

arriving, he was cursing. Said:
All you want will come to you
in a manner you did not wish for.
And the truth is "bounty" — when it came,

unrecognizably, I ac-
knowledge — took me back.

The Unfeeling

In the story you told – that a phantom or *ghost*
(your word, having no other)
sat at the foot of your bed –

                             impression's gist

was the glimmering orb
of the real when
the apparition spoke:

                        You saw through him

(he was translucent), but did he speak your tongue
when he asked what you'd done?
What puny practice, the candle lit, the lover soundly

                              sleeping, the prayer

you incanted with
so much fervor before
you knew him there?

                    Language clicked

against his palate tele-
pathing a power made from
something besides words: *magic* was close to it,

                             your skin shivered

with goose bumps, the door in your wall
of feelings fallen
open, and over-

                 flowing – grief's sudden

                          capacious charge

IV

Sadness remains the source of my politics.
—Alan Michael Parker

austerity

for a while the poor
were poorer for
good measure,
     their treasure
          but leisure,
their days spent
in daze of,
     need for
          (*paid*) –
butter their bread with dust,
drink deep of mourning's mist –
joke about, rescusitant,
as shard of gossip,
     custom of bargain,
          tarried fervescently
The poorer poored
and *nothing too much*
baulked
(a budget was
     a budget that
          wouldn't budge)
while all fall:
     refuse
          accumulate
stink of blank
     looks, windows
          leaden with
cuts of
     glass for
          (imprison'd light)

FORECLOSURE

I was leaving the large house for good.
Melody from an upstairs bedroom
wavered down to me:

I didn't look.
I'd so often woken to a voice,
a vibration, saying over and over,

You have a few minutes. This is a test.
What had I felt from that bed?   Certainly
not fear. But there was never music before.

The living room stretched above me
like a vault. Floors shone darkly,
and it was dark by the door.

SENTIMENTAL

I read for "sediment"
"sentiment." For "matter"
"mental" (feelings).
At which point this picture:
a bear with a ring
through its snout
about to be baited.
Tight shot on dim eyes,
place unlocatable, the appeal
of emotion – pity – to open
pockets. I can't look,
but the knowledge that I can (do)
turn the page turns to living
knowing that the heart may succumb,
suddenly, perhaps inexplicably, to
sentiment for sentient
beings, that the practice
of delivering pain to take
pleasure stops by giving
money. The power
of its appeal lies
in the purse of the righteous.

THE CAYADUTTA CREEK SUITE

I spell — Cayudeta —
phonetically:
               "Cayadutta" *is* English
         spelling for the Mohawk
"stone standing out of water,"
a boulder in the creek
at the foot of the Adirondacks
moved to build the Erie Canal,

long after the Mohawks themselves
moved (forced). The creek was power
source for the leather mills and
               plants growing "like
         weeds along its rocky bed":
tannins used to cure the many hides
to make the gloves of Gloversville
stank. The creek was a gutter.

My high school's nature club
cleaned a stretch of the Cayadutta
               as a class project: tires, a sink,
         orange scum all over. Many condoms.
"Those who lived on
the creek commented on
the water's color based on
what dyes were dumped in."

∞

Smell indelible in memory's ol-
factories. *Like weeds along creek bed.*

∞

The earth as a site.
Earth in our sights.

∞

Release "various gaseous":
the process by which a
              plant whose cell walls
       exchange CO_2 "by auto-
trophic consumption to produce
O_2 is life-
sustaining": generous

in generation is the earth
of emanative commerce –
              water (as vapor), hydro-
       chloride, radium, also
including helium –
these parts of
the planet's exhalation, photo-

synthesis its inhalation.
We do not produce
              oxygen but

release carbon. To
release is not to exchange
but slowly to choke.
I am choking.

∞

Living things recognize life, over-
look dying matter, which is *dispirited*.

∞

1920s: Cayadutta sprang clear from Bleecker
Mountain; deadened along its course.

∞

1970s: the toll to the creek
the mills took stopped.
            Stopped the stench.
      The Cayadutta became
"more associated with young
fisherman catching trout" (stocked).
The mills closed and overnight
the county had the state's lowest

per capita income. No work. No
shops or markets. Downtown died.
            That we shopped in dying

stores. That labor was
not local (moved to Philippines).
That I knew the unemployed as
well as owners moving shop to India.
That I thought nothing of that.

My thoughts were stones
standing out of their depth.
                    That I might now
            see through the waters of
the Cayadutta, smell the burdock,
mullein and sweet grass along
its banks means that there are else-
wheres, other plants, and no one atones.

∞

Caustic plant, pitcher plant, rubber plant,
sensitive plant, spider plant, woody plant, etc.

∞

Vengeance

It raves along a road,
pounds a car with fists,
hollows a face into the roof.
Its spitting image.

And in the woods when an overhanging
darkness of leaves convinces
the air is right,
it raves like a mark branded
by two prongs on a trunk

about the body it collected in parts:
the seat of the pants, skin of the teeth,
the hair's breath sealed now in canning jars
lined up along the cellar wall.
It's all done, all guilty,

and now there is no light.
Pieceably it buries
the skeleton key, that which
it gravely hunted,
loomed raven for.

THE PASSIVIST

Give you a lift? You the helpful man to
stop and offer me a ride to wherever
I must go. So tall I fold into your car.
Now we're arrived – parking lot, blue
barrier wall – at the warehouse. Inside
it's killing you: the crime of being kind.
I turn before you die – regard the trickle
of sunbeam coming through high windows
and down the empty shelves. Insensible.
An open door across the room's too far.
Now that you're dead will they kill me
too? Why didn't I scream, *Stop, murder?*
I stood fear-silenced. If your death's real –
but I can't say – guilt has unspoken me.

ON PRINCIPLE

*I asked a Kantian, "Does this mean that, if I don't give myself
Kant's Imperative as a law, I am not subject to it?" "No," I was
told, "you have to give yourself a law, and there is only one law."*
—Derek Parfit

Is an act unprincipled
      because it's not subject
            to one law? A principle's
optimistic (the outlawed plan
      might not be under-
            taken). Also realistic:
it's will whether to
      do or resist doing
            something desired,
like a forbidden love,
      or deliberated,
            as the law allows,
like a necessary killing.
      The act could be refused,
            an error of ways, erratic
and wayward, the self
      lost in the moment of action,
            yet at the same time,
fulfilled. In mind,
      on the mind, neither
            certainty nor satiety.
Who really wants to weather
      the way a gobbled meal
            holds the body,

hiccups insisting on
        presence before the sleep-
           inducing tryptophan
of food takes effect,
        or believe killing could make us
           just, something other
than killers, or bestow a peace
        that may cometh at last
           because we haven't done
everything, right or wrong,
        we dreamed of, that
           arresting ourselves
being in principle a choice,
        though we'll never even
           now (say it!) say it?

SMALL MAHOGANY TABLE WITH VOICE

(the poet H.D. in London, 1944)

The point of the Home Circle at
all — the "all" of a séance —
was science. We thought it
                    psychic research,

holding hands in the dark as
we waited for veritable signs.
When the table, a friend's gift,
                    and she dead in

a raid, moved, we knew.
It knocked (tapped).
We sat rapt. Now no one
                    could doubt

the truth: *War over*
in November (sly words for
our greatest hope!). Clarified:
                    War over after

the elections (slyer still). When
one of us was alone the table
came alive (we took
                    her word),

tap dancing until she hunched
in secret in the cold room in a daze
day and night dreaming of saving
                    the world with

a message that realized
the integument of the living
was our bond with the dead.
                    Not bond,

but *bomb*. A kind of spirit-
play by association we could not read.
Then we could: *war war war*
                    until the end.

The Blizzard

I looked for the room I was booked in
for one thing or another we say we'll do
and regret when the time comes the unlooked-for
encounters with black ice, the kind strangers offering
a hand up. A gallery with high ceilings and windows.
I wandered blank as a snowdrift.

There were candelabra scattered about
on oak sideboards. Someone lit real candles
because the lights had gone out.
The aromatic flames of beeswax,
the golden flickers of risibility
with their cold blue hearts.

I happened upon a grand staircase widening
down to the hall. Marble, that polished,
shone translucent. *Hello*, I called,
looking at someone near the foot of the stairs
about to leave. *What*
should I be doing? My arms stretched out like wings,

white, almost diaphanous my blouse.
Everyone I'd seen was white, actually,
which I'd have thought strange,
except I did not think about it until now.
The stairway a dead giveaway: All the labor
to build it, the anonymity of the work,

the scarring of the mahogany bannister,
as if hundreds of sharpened nails
had scored the railing over the years. The person below left,
and I clapped, a curtain having fallen.
I should go, too. Into the tense
sudden silence of blizzard, the whiteout.

FLUFF

for L.K.C.

Of pollen freed
    from anther drifts
        into woods, what
naturalists term
    "a troubled landscape"
        and you call "beautiful."
Somewhere
    you knew that
        humans trouble
all we touch
    though that
        was intuition.
To translate farms,
    houses, sheep
        and cows, cities,
sewers, power
    stations, satellites,
        spies, the grab for
power like the grab
    for mineral rights:
        humans cannot
stand uncertain
    or imaginary
        gain. You think,
imagination has
    no power. Yet
        what else makes

our feelings sway
       and moves us
              with such force
we wake up as
       if (your case)
              from near-
death: a cave that
       yawned before
              you, *abra-*
cadaver, and
       something (some-
              one) murmured,
Only flesh
       knows love
              my love.
Your one foot
       lifted to cross
              over, one
eye opening to
       stay, and *now*
              the reason why.

The Sibyl

. . . man's genius is one of lies.
—after Nietzsche

Presume
mirrored
reflection.

Vastly you
do not thyself
know:

& don't believe
me am I
right?

To seek the source,
that steep alley of
stone,

to make the long
climb to thatched hut to find what's
what,

to encounter
reality's
prismed:

a window of light, corner of fire,
the crone's
inscrutable

smile when you fill
the door with your big Western
boots.

Don't mistake her
trembling for
welcome

though it's fruitful to have everything
afraid of
you:

So accidental
an Occidental insight you think it has no
consequence

you forgive gaffs,
those verbal arrows of unerring
erring

that violate reason in
language hiding
intent,

having long lost the capacity
for perception of anyone else's individual
will,

but consider the poor
overlooked
conscience

is a trait which you have
observed humans occasionally to
use.

V

One might speak of a life
or a moment as "unforgettable"
even if all men had forgotten it.
　　—Walter Benjamin

In Place of Feelings

We enter the compound as foreigners the compound empty of others from our tour and also the others who once lived in the narrow open cubicles with thin walls on which fastened short slabs of beds no one could sleep on, cramped, riddled with lice, coughing breathless as those who, punched, cannot breathe. Everything's dust-covered, little plaques of history so many old stories the eyes narrow. *They're here,* my friend says, *I feel them their sorrow's relentless,* and relentlessly she's shaking, feeling them. I feel nothing. No. I judge only how there was no mercy that here hearts burst.

ELEGY WITH BOULDER

No trees. At dusk, seven deer caught in silhouette. Beside them, the boulder that was my father, large as a town, discrete, a hillock, grass-mired, granite shoved through basalt. I stood in its shadow, nearing it then stopping. My hands felt along a surface I couldn't see, as if glass barred me from touching it. Above me, a vaulting midnight space struck with feathers of clouds. They'd dynamited the boulder the week before. Nothing moved it. Equipment broke. Eventually, they built the road around the boulder. I thought I'd find a door if I tarried. My hands moved in circles wider and wider seeking sides like walls in a room. No sides or entrance. Certainly, no *way*.

THE WALKING WOMAN OF LEWISBURG, PA

Reached the birch tree lightning broke, cracked, split, now dry beyond repair, cast toward a terse, blue sky, birds sailing on wind's wing in silhouette. Thought to fly with my dog back home but stopped by a woman I've seen walking far along the two-lane highway in and out of town, on alleys (never streets). Striding, a slip of a person, bent as if skating into a stiff wind all the days of the year, who for whatever reason can't relent, until the moment stayed her: my dog, she told me, reminded her of her own whole-cloth loss — twin huskies, husband, house — unspooled her on the road, face the ruddy hue of autumn apples left lying on the ground after first frost.

Outside of London (July 1981)

for the Erickson sisters

They went instead to walk
a road or meadow with asters along the fence:
A turn near her sister
and the way before her
blocked by what felt solid
but was invisible

Their shadows overhung with apple branch
and small green fruit obscured a gate —
called in the guidebook "the kissing gate" —
lodged
in a scrim
of leaves

The gate separated the path
from a field of cows clover
and flies in their aureolic buzzing hovered
circled about her sister's head
the whole length of the pasture
into which they climbed over the turnstile

Her sister asked *Is it far?*
There was a Viking wall
or vault   She'd seen a sign
and said *We're there soon*
as the crow
is a hallowed bird

In a moment framed by larch which border memory the sisters speak,
still —

In/Visible

Mother speaks to her mother of air
(her mother who's not here).
She asks me, *Can't you see her?*

I see the clock, the chair,
the tea in teacups as my mother
speaks to her mother of air.

She first spoke with her mother after
two falls and the illness-onset but before
the stroke. She asks, Can't you see her?

Take me home, Mother, my mother
says to the room. If you're
speaking to Grandma, say that I miss her,

I call. Her whole life she never
ordered her mother. Now, *Mother,*
she commands the air. *Can't you see her?*

I want the pain over forever.
What's the rush? I chide her
who speaks to her mother of air,
though I cannot see her.

OFFHANDED

1

I hold a glass that flies
  from my
  hand. I
catch it. Fumble. Spill
  it over. My hands
  drop the glass again.
I can explain flying things
  as illness that
  ravaged wrist.
When I grip to shake
  hands now I do
  not grip. I lift
the glass which is half-full
  to sip: water drops —
  splash face.

2

What should I
  think? My arm has
  withered over
time, it's true. Walking
  quickly through
  the house I run my hand
five times into chairs and walls,
  as if it's someone else's
  that my muscles don't

control. Emaciate
         wrist no longer bends.
         I don't care.
Not care
         but mind. How
         should I feel other-
wise? The ceiling
         doesn't cry.
         Face dry.

                3

What wakes me up
         at 3am's invisible
         but sharp: Pain,
you get
         around! clutch
         me closer
in your grip than
         any lover,
         freeze me life
and limb. To tell the Night
         the truth is small
         relief from
it. Chance baptized
         me, but Pain
         anoints its own.

Care Giving: An Elegy

You hold the hand, perfectly still, with all your strength. Surely, if you can only
try hard enough, something will move and live again, something will revive.
—Variation on a quotation from Margaret Atwood's *Bodily Harm*

The windows in the room in which you are giving care are storm
and once filled with flies so many bluebottles caught against
spring's light Father gathered them gently, in tissue, to clear the air

> of all the buzzing motes of night
> he then cast into the March wind.
> You – raise your voice to be heard

∞

in the small room with the large marriage bed with the marriage bed-
spread which is stained with all manner of
memories shadowing the pieces of mind and the making peace with what has been

> done or said – all, now,
> done. *I was stroking his arm*
> *and the soft hair bent as I stroked*

∞

and that is how I knew he was alive
then the hair unbending
and his skin cooling –

> *What's happening?* she asked
> Mother grimaces inside her stare
> out the window at the green

fields and finding such an effort
to form words to express her experience of
Whitman's spirit's transcendence which she cannot

avow: *The whole afternoon*
and the next day the cat in the crook of
my arm channeled your father —

∞

the words welling from
the failings of aged nerves
to blunt their charge:

raw, and her voice's sudden
agony: *What am I*
going to do?

∞

She is an *I* who can
no longer read hear
or walk and *he* —

her ears, cane, brain —
was dying his hand
was in yours

(Did you just say,
she turned at that moment to ask,
We love you? We love you?)

Last night you startled at a sound rose from deep sleep expectant —
to the empty air. She awakened too not straining at all to hear something, or
more.

ELEGY WITH WINDOW

for my father

Arms crossed as in —
          dearth of
                   beating heart — the heart
                           now cradled (clay):

turn to me you turned like a sunflower toward
light from the window Mother sat by
               then you could not oh
                   you cannot move
                       or anymore see
someone you loved
seeing YOU passing into that space of
           (~~life~~)
                   shifting the negative
                       ions your absence
generates in not being
            Aware of
               that desire for
                   this deliberate attention:

Your daughter leaning to touch
then touching in awkward last embrace
           Placing hands
               on either side of
                   your face

ELEGY WITH LAKE

The lake's marine blue,
with little whitecaps from wind.
A small granite outcrop borders
the shore (the lake has no beach).
There's no swimming on this day
or at least in this scene, which is true
in simple detail. *Tell me a story from your life,*
my dead father asks (he can still speak in poems),

but to say so I add his voice
addressing *me,*
and now remove it.
Everything shifts:
That day I could swim with my father.
From the rock where I sat, the lake was deep, its water like ink.
I wanted to swim. I always swam. I thought to swim
with my father but he stayed in the boat.

In truth he wasn't there because he hated the water.
Has everything changed
with the declaration of fact? Voice,
mood—the addition
of someone who is not at all
the sum of a million such moments, like nothing, or nothing more.
This, my father says, *was my good fortune, but in another time, and at a lake*
that ineffably persists, call it The Lake of Happily, in which I dipped my foot, dove.

CLEARLY IN FALL

for my mother

Stones are not stars,
she thinks.
What will I know?

Autumn glasses over.
To hands
that hold her

back at last she cries
—*No more love*—
and casts them off.

Now can she tousle
free of
tree tops at the forest's edge,

where leaves may vary,
but the mountain's
not so much green,

orange and gold
as humble.
That clarity.

Notes

Part I

"Spirit Says (2)": Some quoted material drawn from the *OED* (on-line version).

Part II

"Interview with a Samizdat Poet": Slava Yastremski is a professor of Russian Language and Literature at Bucknell University. The original interview was held at The Poet's Cottage on the Bucknell campus on September 15, 1999. The poem is dedicated to Slava and also to the poet, Olga Sedakova, with great thanks for their permission to redeploy some of the tattered remnants from our interview in this poem.

Part III

"On Securities and Exchange": includes a line from Pamela Stewart.

"In the Space-Time Studio of Morgan O": Some of the quoted portions are drawn from email exchanges between the artist and the author (2010), and some from a review of featured artist Morgan O'Hara's Live Transmission Drawing Performance at The LAB Gallery (New York), by Elizabeth Torres, published in the *Red Door Magazine*, Issue 3 (2010). Online journal available at www.reddoormag.com.

"At the Lawrence Ranch": "Sturdy snow" is how the California-based poet, Devreaux Baker, described hail when seeing it for the first time. The quoted line, "the tree-trunk there like a guardian An-gel," is quoted from the Lawrence Ranch brochure.

"At the Agnes Martin Gallery": I was told by the gallery director that I could not quote any of the Agnes Martin material in the Agnes Martin Gallery catalogue or legends, so I have only quoted the gallery director herself. Some quotations, however, are drawn from the exhibition catalogue for *3 x Abstraction: New Methods of Drawing by Hilma af Klint, Emma Kunz, and Agnes Martin,* at The Drawing Center in 2005. Catalogue edited by Catherine de Zegher and Hendel Teicher (Yale University Press and The Drawing Center, 2005).

"The Unfeeling": The line "Language clicked against his palate" is from Virginie Lalucq's serial poem, *Fortino Sámano* (2004). Trans-lated by the author.

PART IV

"The Cayadutta Creek Suite": Some portions of this poem are drawn from and quote the article by Keith A. Kvenvolden and Bruce W. Rogers: "Gaia's breath—global methane exhalations." *Marine and Petroleum Geology* 22 (2005): 579–590. http://walrus.wr.usgs.gov/reports/reprints/Kvenvolden_MPG22.pdf.

Other portions of the poem are drawn from an article in my home-town's local paper: Kayleigh Karutis, "Quiet Cayadutta." *The Leader Herald*. May 17, 2009. http://www.leaderherald.com/page/content.detail/id/512462/Quiet-Cayadutta.html.

And Fulton County Historian: R. M. Palmer, M. D., "Without Cayadutta Creek Gloversville Would Now Be Section of Kingsborough." 1949. http://fulton.nygenweb.net/history/glovcayadutta.html.

"On Principle": The epigraph is quoted from "How to Be Good," by Larissa MacFarquhar, an article about the Oxford philosopher Derek Parfit on page 49 of *The New Yorker* from September 5, 2011. The poem draws very loosely (and inaccurately) on the language, perhaps the ideas described, in this article.

"Small Mahogany Table with Voice": Quoted portions are from H.D.'s "séance notes" from Spiritualist sessions she attended during WWII (housed in the Beinecke Library at Yale University). The poem is for Elizabyth Hiscox.

PART V

"In Place of Feelings" is for Pamela Uschuk.

"Outside of London (July 1981)" is for my mother, Vange, and her beloved sisters—Char, Syl, and Doie.